tea with
wisdom

A Collection of Poems Inspired
by the Old Testament

Christina Van Starkenburg

BOOKS BY CHRISTINA VAN STARKENBURG

The Divided Realm Trilogy

The Key Thief
Secret Beneath the Stone (Coming Soon)

Picture Books

One Tiny Turtle: A Story You Can Colour
Anne's Adventure: A Pirate's ABCs
Annika's Imaginary Friend (Coming Soon)

Text copyright © 2022 by Christina Van Starkenburg

All rights reserved. The use of any part this publication reproduced, transmitted in any form or by any means, electronic, mechanical, photocopying, recording, or otherwise, or stored in a retrieval system, without the prior consent of the author is an infringement of the copyright law.

To contact the author, visit her at
www.christinavanstarkenburg.com

Title: Praying Through the Old Testament
Names: Van Starkenburg, Christina, author, illustrator
Description: A collection of poems inspired by each book in the Old Testament.

Hardcover ISBN: 9798833423998
Paperback ISBN: 9798817907339

Cover designed by GetCovers.

All Scripture quotations, unless otherwise indicated, are taken from the Holy Bible, Today's New International Version™ TNIV. ® Copyright © 2001, 2005 by International Bible Society®. All rights reserved worldwide.

Scripture quotations marked (ESV) are from the ESV Bible (The Holy Bible, English Standard Version®), copyright © 2001 by Crossway, a publishing ministry of Good News Publishers. All rights reserved.

*For Grandpa.
You inspired more of these poems
than you will ever know.
I love you and I miss you.*

Contents

Preface ix

Part One: Pentateuch

Breathe Life in This World	3
Like Adam and Eve	4
Ark and Rainbow	6
You Said Go	7
Sometimes, You Want Us to Wait	8
The Lord Will Provide	9
Favoured	10
The Story of Joseph	11
A Job for Us	12
The Red Sea	14
The 10 Commandments	15
Gifts for the Creator God	18
Wayyiqra	20
Honey and Death	21
The Written Word	22
Your Baskets are Blessed	23

Part Two: History

Let Me Be Like Rahab	27
Kingless	28
Broken and Bitter	29

Young Samuel	31
Mirror	32
Jonathan and David	33
The Cavern Home	34
Cedar Gifts of Praise	35
Parenting Prophets	36
Two Piles of Dirt	37
Temple Plans	38
Temple Dedication	40
Destroyed	41
Rebuilding from the Rubble Up	43
Build Together	45
In Royal Gardens	46

PART THREE: BOOKS OF EVERYDAY WISDOM

Hope-Tinged Grief	49
Psalm 86	50
Tea with Wisdom	51
Daily Bread	52
The River of Life	54
A Love Poem	55

PART FOUR: MAJOR PROPHETS

Directionally Challenged	59
On My Heart	60
Coral on the Stone: A Lament	61
For Your Holy Name	63
Faithful and True	64

PART FIVE: THE BOOK OF THE TWELVE

Covenantal Rain	69
Rend Your Heart	70
Just Ash	72
The Bystander Effect	73
Love Our Wayward Feet	74
Micah 6:8	75
Judgement/Comfort	76
Carrier Pigeon Prayers	78
Child's Play	79
Palace of Muck	80
Lead-Covered Basket	81
How Have I Loved You?	83

Preface

I never thought that these poems would end up bound in a book, but here we are. It's been an absolute delight to write them, and I have loved hearing from all of my readers about how these poems have touched them.

As you can probably imagine, there are a few poems that have a special meaning for me, like "Hope-Tinged Grief." This poem came to me in a moment when I needed it. For those of you who weren't along for the original journey, that might sound funny. Because obviously I could have written the poem whenever I needed it. However, when I first started working on this collection, I had committed to working my way through the Old Testament book by book and sending out one poem a week to my newsletter subscribers. And, because I didn't want to let anyone down, I wrote the poems a month a head of time.

This meant I reached the book of Job a week after my grandfather died. Job 19:25-27, the passage that this poem is inspired by was the text they read at Grandpa's funeral.

But that's not the only poem Grandpa inspired. He also shows up in "On My Heart." When we would visit my grandparents in the summer, he would always lead the mealtime prayers. For each prayer he would begin "Our Father who art in heaven, we come to Thee today…" which is the start of this poem. I can't actually read that sentence without hearing him say it. It brings me comfort to know that in this small way he's still here with me.

If you're mourning the loss of someone, I hope you find comfort in these poems. And, if you're not, I hope that you find a treasure in these words as well.

With love,
Christina

Part One:
Pentateuch

BREATHE LIFE IN THIS WORLD

In the beginning God created the heavens and the earth.
Genesis 1:1

You created the sun, the moon, and the stars
All of the planets like Mercury, Venus, and Mars.

The sky up above, the sea down below,
All of the flowers and fruits that can grow.

The sea teems with fish, dolphins, and squids,
Blowing bubbles of delight for the life that they live.

The birds of the sky and the rocks on the ground
Sing of Your praises; a marvelous sound.

You spoke and the animals all came to be
The deer and the bunnies, and the ones I don't see

You didn't stop there, though some may believe
That the world would be perfect if you'd just let it be

Instead, you molded the earth, like a potter with clay
Breathed breath in my lungs, so to you I can pray
And thank you for all you've created, back then, and today.

LIKE ADAM AND EVE

Then the man and his wife heard the sound of the LORD God as he was walking in the garden in the cool of the day, and they hid from the LORD God among the trees of the garden. But the LORD God called to the man, "Where are you?"
Genesis 3:8-9

I'm sorry I sinned.
Like Adam and Eve,
I've messed up again.

I hid from you Lord,
Though my offense is exposed.
Behind branches I cower,
Think my garden is closed.

You know when I sit.
When I rise. When I sleep.
There's not a secret,
From you, I could keep.

Still, I try hiding.
My shame is too great
To admit that I failed
Like it's sealed my fate.

But you walk through the garden
And you call me by name.
Though you know all my crimes,
You let me explain.

I'm sorry I sinned.
But, like Adam and Eve
I try not to admit
That I am the cause of this horrible rift.

When I finally confess it,
Spread my brokenness bare,
You're quick to forgive me,
My curse is one you've chosen to bear.

On the cross,
When you breathed last and died,
My nakedness, once and for all
You chose to forgive and to hide.

Ark and Rainbow

And God said, "This is the sign of the covenant I am making between me and you and every living creature with you, a covenant for all generations to come: I have set my rainbow in the clouds, and it will be the sign of the covenant between me and the earth."
Genesis 9:12-13

Across the sky your
Rainbow shines. Basking us in knowledge that you
Keep your promises.

Although life may be hard, we know
Never again will a flood
Drench the earth; burying mountains like clams in the sand
Removing our sins
And cleansing the land.

I want to be like
Noah, his sons, and their wives,
Bowing down before you, no fear of disdain,
Once more coming to
Worship and adore you.

You Said Go

So Abram went, as the Lord had told him.
Genesis 12:4a

You told Abram to leave his home
Say goodbye to all he had known.
And so, he went on his way,
No thoughts leading him astray.
Finding shalom every day.

Could I follow where you lead me?
Anywhere you call me to be?
Or, would I want to stay here,
With everyone I hold dear,
Acting carefree every year?

I pray I'll be courageous, brave,
And true. You're not my grave,
I long to fully trust you.
To walk, love, and be pursued.
Trust the peace you give, and be made new.

Sometimes, You Want Us to Wait

Now the LORD was gracious to Sarah as he had said, and the LORD did for Sarah what he had promised. Sarah became pregnant and bore a son to Abraham in his old age, at the very time God had promised him.
Genesis 21:1-2

Sometimes, you want us to wait,
Like Abraham looking forward to his blessing:
A child, who seemed to be coming too late.
Sometimes, you want us to wait.
"Patience," you say. But it makes us irate;
We don't want to be left in this state of stressing.
Sometimes, you want us to wait,
Like Abraham looking forward to his blessing.

Abraham waited, watched and prepared,
For a gift from you, Lord:
A child—proof for Sarah, you cared.
Abraham waited, watched and prepared.
But like Sarah, I've often despaired.
With your help, to Abraham's stance I'll move toward:
Abraham waited, watched and prepared,
For a gift from you, Lord.

THE LORD WILL PROVIDE

Abraham looked up and there in a thicket he saw a ram caught by its horns. He went over and took the ram and sacrificed it as a burnt offering instead of his son. So Abraham called that place The LORD Will Provide. And to this day it is said, "On the mountain of the LORD it will be provided."
Genesis 22:13-14

Once we've received your promise
It can feel like we're done.
The waiting is over;
We have our metaphorical son.

But you want to remind us
That this gift is from you.
And so, you call us and test us
To ensure our love is true.

Do we go to the mountain?
Believe we'll meet with you there?
Or do we take what you've promised
And hide it with care?

I ask you for the courage,
To set aside all my pride,
So I can meet you on the mountain,
The Lord will Provide.

Favoured

Isaac, who had a taste for wild game, loved Esau, but Rebekah loved Jacob.
Genesis 25:28

Invisible bruises are left under our skin
When we, and others, let favouritism in.

First Jacob and Esau, a brotherhood, severed
Then Rachel and Leah, a love broken forever.

The boys' parents took sides, chose the son they loved best,
Led them to trickery to change the one who was blessed.

Like mother, like son, Jacob took what he learned
In how he treated his wives: one loved and one spurned.

It hurts, and it shows in the way the siblings relate
To be the one less loved and rejected; our hearts just deflate.

Heavenly Father, help us know that when we feel burned
By someone's careful, careless choice that makes our hearts yearn

That you, faithful Father, have reached into this mess,
Favoured us all. Each one of us blessed.

THE STORY OF JOSEPH

But Joseph said to them, "Don't be afraid. Am I in the place of God? You intended to harm me, but God intended it for good to accomplish what is now being done, the saving of many lives. So then, don't be afraid. I will provide for you and your children." And he reassured them and spoke kindly to them.
Genesis 50:19-21

I sometimes feel like Joseph.
I've gone
From lavish gowns to prison robes
From favoured son to slave.
I don't take it
With nearly as much grace.
I have not learned
To be content
Whatever is my lot
I wonder
And I ask you why
You've left me here to rot.
Help me
Learn to trust you
To believe this is in your plan
Even if it's decades
Before I see
How my life is in your hands.

A Job For Us

But Moses said to the Lord, "Oh, my Lord, I am not eloquent, either in the past or since you have spoken to your servant, but I am slow of speech and of tongue." Then the Lord said to him, "Who has made man's mouth? Who makes him mute, or deaf, or seeing, or blind? Is it not I, the Lord? Now therefore go, and I will be with your mouth and teach you what you shall speak." Exodus 4:10-12 (ESV)

Before we were born
You had a plan
That you whisper in our ears
On winds we barely can hear.
Or burn before our eyes
In bushes that do not die.

Then, you wait for our response.
                But Moses said
And I can echo
          "My Lord,
          I am not eloquent,
          I am slow of speech and tongue."
Is that not often the way?
We doubt we are the one.

          The Lord said to him,
To me
To all of us
          "Who has made man's mouth?
          Who makes him mute,

>   deaf,
>   seeing,
>   or blind?
>   Is it not I, the Lord?"
A rhetorical question
Has just one answer
That I do not want to hear or see.

>   "Now go.
>   I will be with your mouth
>   and teach you
>   what you shall speak."
And yet, I still resist.

>   Then the Lord's anger burned
For this quest
That I've spurned.
But still, You do not give up
You make a way
To support and aid
While we build our confidence up.

THE RED SEA

Then the LORD *said to Moses, "Why are you crying out to me? Tell the Israelites to move on. Raise your staff and stretch out your hand over the sea to divide the water so that the Israelites can go through the sea on dry ground."*
Exodus 14:15-16

The wind howled through the sea.
The water stood on end.
A dry path appeared between these water walls
Perilous from its start until its end.
Here is where you bade them walk;
They must trust you once again.

To us, that trust seems easy,
We know how the story goes:
They just saw ten miracles
As you wrenched them from their foes.
But would we act any differently
If you call us out into the sea?

THE 10 COMMANDMENTS

"The most important one," answered Jesus, "is this: 'Hear, O Israel: The Lord our God, the Lord is one. Love the Lord your God with all your heart and with all your soul and with all your mind and with all your strength.' The second is this: 'Love your neighbor as yourself.' There is no commandment greater than these."
Mark 12:29-31

Ten laws summed up in two:
Love the Lord with all your heart, soul, mind, and strength,
And love your neighbour, the same way you love you.

ONE

The first: no other gods before him
Can seem simple to you and me.
But while Isis, Anubis and Horus are foreign,
What gods do we choose before him?

TWO

Make no image at which to bend the knee.
Our God is far to great and unexplainable
To be fashioned into something by you or me.

THREE

Do not misuse his name
With our words, actions or deeds.

He is too pure, too Holy
To let us use his name to fulfill our worldly needs.

FOUR

The seventh day, is a day of rest.
Do we treat it well?
And show our love for him (and us)
As we relax and, with him, let our thoughts dwell?

FIVE

Honour your father and mother, love and treat them well.
When they are imperfect, remember:
We were all broken when Eve and Adam fell.

SIX

Do not kill
Or let your anger win.
They share the same root,
They are the same sin.

SEVEN

Don't take lightly the gift of sex,
Though we may think differently,
Maybe we should admit that He does know best.

EIGHT

Don't take things that are not yours;
Give freely from what you have.
In God's world there is enough for all
We just need to open up our hands.

Nine

Do not lie. It's a disease
Spread quickly with a tongue.
It ruins the lives and hopes and dreams
Of the one your cruelty has undone.

Ten

Do not want what you don't have
Be content, right where you are.
Trust in the Lord, he knows your needs
He will always be right where you are.

Ten laws summed up in two:
Love the Lord with all your heart, soul, mind, and strength,
And love your neighbour, the same way you love you.

GIFTS FOR THE CREATOR GOD

Then the Lord said to Moses, "See, I have chosen Bezalel son of Uri, the son of Hur, of the tribe of Judah, and I have filled him with the Spirit of God, with wisdom, with understanding, with knowledge and with all kinds of skills—to make artistic designs for work in gold, silver and bronze, to cut and set stones, to work in wood, and to engage in all kinds of crafts."
Exodus 31:1-5

Bezalel bent carefully over his task.
Days and months passed
As he laboured over a single piece of art.
Lace-like gold spun from his hands,
Embossing gemstones, plates and bowls
Each bound for the temple of his God.

Long was he a master of his craft,
He'd studied and practiced it for years.
But now, his hands were truly blest
For God saw the love within his heart
And chose him, Bezalel, for this special part.

Designs with gold, silver, and bronze
Came to him like waking dreams.
Each piece he fashioned, was truly art
A gift of love for his God above
A creator, just like him.

Heavenly Father, let us use
The gifts you've given us.

Let us study the crafts we love
The things you've placed upon our hearts.
You might not bless us like Bezalel
Help us know that's okay.
For when we offer our works to you,
You'll treasure them always.

WAYYIQRA[1]

You are to be holy to me because I, the LORD, am holy, and I have set you apart from the nations to be my own.
Leviticus 20:26

He called them to be
Holy, as He is Holy.
They are set apart
Claimed as His treasured people
But, they must follow His laws.

This call, it echoes
Across the generations
Throughout time and place
In our hearts, this call takes root
Nudging us to be holy

But do we listen?
Do we let the message in?
And try to follow
His two rules, to show our love
For Him, and those around us?

I hope His love shines
Through my life and blesses those
Who live around me.
My heart longs to be holy,
The way He called me to be.

---

[1] wayyiqra (Way-E-Kra) is the Hebrew title of Leviticus. It is the first word of the text and it means "And he called."

Honey and Death

They gave Moses this account: "We went into the land to which you sent us, and it does flow with milk and honey! Here is its fruit. But the people who live there are powerful, and the cities are fortified and very large. We even saw descendants of Anak there... We can't attack those people; they are stronger than we are." And they spread among the Israelites a bad report about the land they had explored. They said, "The land we explored devours those living in it."
Numbers 13:27-28, 31-32

Outside the wall
I stand and stare
I tremble in fear
What waits for me there.

You promise good things
Honey and life
And the reports that come back
Show me that is right.

But I listen to rumors,
To lies and untruths
They tell me I'll fail
They say, these sooths

Help me let you prevail
Shine through their lies
Let me enter the land
The way you advise.

The Written Word

When he takes the throne of his kingdom, he is to write for himself on a scroll a copy of this law, taken from that of the Levitical priests.
Deuteronomy 17:18

The King
Must read the Book of Laws
Every single day. He
Must write it word for word.
So in his heart it stays.

May we
Follow his example
Write God's word on our hearts
By reading it daily
Memorizing each part.

Your Baskets Are Blessed

Your basket and your kneading trough will be blessed.
Deuteronomy 28:5

Your baskets are blessed
When God's laws you obey.
Your baking and making
Will prosper each day.
The Lord will establish
The works of your hands.
When you listen to Him
He will bless the whole land.

Part Two:
History

LET ME BE LIKE RAHAB

So she sent them away, and they departed. And she tied the scarlet cord in the window.
Joshua 2:21

Let me be like Rahab
With her scarlet cord,
Who, though it is dangerous,
Risks everything for you Lord.

Let me be like Rahab,
Who barters for her life,
With her wit and wisdom
Asks for what she knows is right.

Let me be like Rahab,
Who sees when you are near,
And trusts that this upheaval
Will only make you clearer.

KINGLESS

In those days Israel had no king; everyone did as they saw fit.
Judges 21:25

In those days Israel had no king,
No one to guide their path.
Each man and woman on their own
Decided what was best.

In these days we have a king
But do we know his name?
Or do each and everyone of us
Follow Israel towards their shame?

Let us listen to our Judge,
Not just once or twice,
But with each breath and every step
So he can guide us right.

BROKEN AND BITTER

"Don't call me Naomi," she told them. "Call me Mara, because the Almighty has made my life very bitter. I went away full, but the LORD has brought me back empty. Why call me Naomi? The LORD has afflicted me; the Almighty has brought misfortune upon me."
Ruth 1:20-21

Broken and bitter,
Like Mara, I come.
Inside is empty,
My hope is undone.

Where are you, Lord,
When the hard times are here?
Where are you, Lord?
Why don't you feel near?

Broken, still trusting,
I call on your name.
But, still, I falter.
Will I feel full again?

Where are you, Lord,
When the hard times are here?
Where are you, Lord?
Why don't you feel near?

Broken. I listen,
To your call on the wind,

It caresses my cheek;
Kindles hope once again.

YOUNG SAMUEL

And the boy Samuel continued to grow in stature and in favor with the LORD and with people.
1 Samuel 2:26

And he grew in strength and favour
Of both men and God
Serving you right from his youth
In your house he trod

This is my prayer for my sons
And my daughter too
That they would grow to love you more
And learn to be like you

Let them grow in favour
Of both God and men
Let them serve you from their youth
Not just now and then

MIRROR

But the LORD said to Samuel, "Do not consider his appearance or his height, for I have rejected him. The LORD does not look at the things human beings look at. People look at the outward appearance, but the LORD looks at the heart."
1 Samuel 16:7

In the mirror I see myself,
With looks I wish to change.
Why would anyone choose me at all?
Surely, You must feel the same.

But, You look at neither
Appearance or height.
To you, they matter not.
For what's important is within.
It's all within my heart.

Do I long to follow You,
To serve the way you want?
Do I love the way You love?
Am I a mirror of your heart?

JONATHAN AND DAVID

Jonathan said to David, "Go in peace, for we have sworn friendship with each other in the name of the LORD, saying, 'The LORD is witness between you and me, and between your descendants and my descendants forever.'" Then David left, and Jonathan went back to the town.
1 Samuel 20:42

When trouble is coming
And dark nights close in
Friends, closer than brothers,
Bring hope once again.

With the shot of an arrow
A message was sent
To run. Flee from the hatred
Of a king whose last love was spent.

Crying, they kissed
As they said their goodbyes.
Parting in peace,
Though, they should be on opposite sides.

When trouble is coming
And dark nights close in
Friends, closer than brothers,
Bring hope once again.

THE CAVERN HOME

David left Gath and escaped to the cave of Adullam. When his brothers and his father's household heard about it, they went down to him there. All those who were in distress or in debt or discontented gathered around him, and he became their commander. About four hundred men were with him.
1 Samuel 22:1-2

Deep green moss grows upon the rocks.
Water trickles down the walls.
The sound, though quiet, echoes there
Throughout the cavern's halls.
But now, the steady dripping sound
Is drowned out by the shuffling feet
Of the caverns many new inhabitants
Who gather round the one that their king seeks.
Four hundred distressed, indebted, discontented souls
Dwell deep within those caves
Close to the man who will be king
At the time when God ordains.
Until that day should come to be,
Not rushed on by their king,
These men chose their cavern home
And make their beds among the moss.

CEDAR GIFTS OF PRAISE

After the king was settled in his palace and the LORD had given him rest from all his enemies around him, he said to Nathan the prophet, "Here I am, living in a house of cedar, while the ark of God remains in a tent."

Nathan replied to the king, "Whatever you have in mind, go ahead and do it, for the LORD is with you."

But that night the word of the LORD came to Nathan, saying: "Go and tell my servant David, 'This is what the LORD says: Are you the one to build me a house to dwell in?'"
2 Samuel 7:1-5

Who are we to give you thanks?
To build you homes of cedar planks?
All we have—it came from you.
You need nothing. What can we do?

Who are you to give us gifts?
To lavish on us until our spirit lifts?
You'd dwell in a tent in the sand or snow
To move with us, where ever we go.

Our Sovereign God, Creator, King.
You love infinitely. You gave us everything.
And so, we turn our praise to you,
It isn't much, but it's all we can do.

Parenting Prophets

When Elijah heard it, he pulled his cloak over his face and went out and stood at the mouth of the cave.

Then a voice said to him, "What are you doing here, Elijah?"
1 Kings 19:13

You work within us, you show us your power
But still, when danger comes, we cower.
We flee from threats. Think you aren't here.
Hide in the wilderness. Beg you to be clearer.

Do you sigh whene'er we flee?
Think to yourself, "You just need to trust me?"
But still, like a parent when their baby cries,
You hold us close, and dry our eyes.
You give us food, and a place to sleep.
You invite us out to hear you speak.
You give us friends to help us out
To remind us of your love; leave us without doubt.

Two Piles of Dirt

"If you will not," said Naaman, "please let me, your servant, be given as much earth as a pair of mules can carry, for your servant will never again make burnt offerings and sacrifices to any other god but the LORD."
2 Kings 5:17

When Naaman had a leprose spot
Elisha bid him in the water wash
Seven times to make him clean
But Naaman thought the idea obscene
At his servants urging he changed his mind
Dipped in the water the seven times
Out he came with skin restored
And a heart to serve Elisha's LORD
Two piles of dirt he brought back home
To worship God upon his throne
He did not know God knew no bounds
He was not tied to Israel's mounds.

Temple Plans

David said, "My son Solomon is young and inexperienced, and the house to be built for the LORD should be of great magnificence and fame and splendor in the sight of all the nations. Therefore I will make preparations for it." So David made extensive preparations before his death.
1 Chronicles 22:5

King David had a simple wish
To build a temple grand
So that all the world would know
That God was in command

But David's dream was not to be
Fulfilled within his life
For God said too much blood was shed
His days were filled with too much strife

Instead, his son Solomon
Would build God's royal home
For there would be a time of peace
While he was on the throne

But David could not just sit
And do nothing for his King
He gave from his great wealth
Silver, gems, and golden rings.

He also took the time to plan
What role the Levities would play

So that when Solomon took the throne
Construction could be started right away

And then he took his child and said,
"Be strong and brave my son.
Build God's home without any fear
He will be here until the work is done."

Temple Dedication

The Lord appeared to him at night and said: "I have heard your prayer and have chosen this place for myself as a temple for sacrifices."
2 Chronicles 7:12

Though You did not need it
Solomon built you up a home.
And you chose to consecrate it
And claimed it as your own.

You promised him, your heart
Your eyes would be forever in that place.
And should the people follow you
They'd forever feel your grace.

That same promise holds us still,
Though the walls are flesh and bone.
For in our hearts is where you dwell
Inside us is your throne.

May we walk with you so faithfully
Like David did before.
Keep all of your decrees and laws
Until we come to heaven's shore.

DESTROYED

This is what Cyrus king of Persia says: "The LORD, the God of heaven, has given me all the kingdoms of the earth and he has appointed me to build a temple for him at Jerusalem in Judah. Any of his people among you—may the LORD their God be with them, and let them go up."
2 Chronicles 36:23

But, Israel's journey was not at an end
They did not listen,
They revelled in sin.

We, too, don't stay worshipping you
We turn our backs to the throne,
Welcome lesser gods in.

And so, you sent them far from their lands
Your temple destroyed
By fire and men

What happens to us when we choose not to obey?
Do you send word to turn us
Hope we trust you once again?

And if we refuse let our dreams be taken away
For years or generations
Until we repent

And can be restored in unexpected ways
Like the Israelites,

Who King Cyrus sent

To their homeland once again.
They could restore their temple to you,
The choice was up to them to return,
The choice is always up to us too.

REBUILDING FROM THE RUBBLE UP

Then Joshua son of Jozadak and his fellow priests and Zerubbabel son of Shealtiel and his associates began to build the altar of the God of Israel to sacrifice burnt offerings on it, in accordance with what is written in the Law of Moses the man of God.
Ezra 3:2

At the rubble, the
Altar was built
And sacrifices made

Because the people knew to
Be humble to
Bring God's blessing once again.

Cedar trees and cymbal sounds
Come together to
Celebrate the sight

Despite dissenting voices
Destruction gave way to new life.
Do we heed their example?

Each one of us has pains, we been
Exiled from our homelands. We long to
Enter once again. Some how me must

Find faith to fumble
Forward on our knees and

Follow our Lord and Saviour.

Go, no matter where he leads.

BUILD TOGETHER

"I and my brothers and my men are also lending the people money and grain. But let us stop charging interest! Give back to them immediately their fields, vineyards, olive groves and houses, and also the interest you are charging them—one percent of the money, grain, new wine and olive oil."

"We will give it back," they said. "And we will not demand anything more from them. We will do as you say."
Nehemiah 5:10-12

Working together
They rebuilt the wall.
With Nehemiah as leader
No one could fall.
He cared for the
Poor, the scared and afraid
Convinced others to help him
Together they raised
People and buildings
Until Jerusalem was restored
A gift for his brothers, sisters, and Lord
When we work together
What will we achieve?
With each building our section
Under a true leader's lead.

IN ROYAL GARDENS

When Esther's words were reported to Mordecai, he sent back this answer: "Do not think that because you are in the king's house you alone of all the Jews will escape. For if you remain silent at this time, relief and deliverance for the Jews will arise from another place, but you and your father's family will perish. And who knows but that you have come to royal position for such a time as this?"
Esther 4:12-14

        Human folly grows like flowers
       When we trust in earthly powers.
   And, like mushrooms growing in gloom
Human prejudices cause irrevocable doom.
     But, while this poisonous plot is set,
    God is still the master gardener yet.
        In the thistles, rocks, and thorns
A young girl planted; with golden laurels adorned.
         With her uncle's guiding hand,
   She saves her people, like God had planned.

Part Three:
Books of Everyday Wisdom

HOPE-TINGED GRIEF

*I know that my redeemer lives,
and that in the end he will stand on the earth.
And after my skin has been destroyed,
yet in my flesh I will see God;
I myself will see him
with my own eyes—I, and not another.
How my heart yearns within me!
Job 19:25-27*

> I know that my redeemer lives:
> You died and rose again.
> Raised on high to your Father's side.
> Your reign will never end.
>
> After my skin has been destroyed,
> Yet, in my flesh I will see your face.
> Though in times when death is near,
> The pain stubbornly remains.
>
> My heart yearns to see Grandpa,
> Who is now standing by your side,
> Thumbing an organ or a snare drum
> Joyously praising you on high.
>
> Someday I will join him,
> See you with my own eyes.
> Someday we will all come before
> In a time when there are no more tears to cry.

PSALM 86

Hear me, LORD, and answer me, for I am poor and needy.
Psalm 86:1

Hear me, Lord, and answer me,
for I am poor and needy.
Everything I thought I had
lies in ashes on the floor.
Bring your servant joy once more,
for I still trust in you.

No one else compares to you
in the heavens or on earth.
You alone deserve my worship
for your glory fills the earth.
Great is the love you have for me,
you deliver me from despair.

Save the daughter
of your daughter.
Fill my heart with hope again
for I fear your name.
Teach me to be like you,
for I long to see your face.

Tea with Wisdom

Out in the open wisdom calls aloud, she raises her voice in the public square.
Proverbs 1:20

        Holy Father, Spirit, and Son,

        Help me not to think I'm wise
           far beyond the truth.
        Help me flee from foolish ways,
           and the follies of my youth.

        Let me heed wisdom's call
        when she knocks upon my heart.
        Empower me to invite her to tea,
        to listen, and let her truth impart.

DAILY BREAD

Two things I ask of you, LORD;
  do not refuse me before I die:
Keep falsehood and lies far from me;
  give me neither poverty nor riches,
  but give me only my daily bread.
Proverbs 30:7-8

Two things Agur asked of you Lord;
  I'm not sure I'd do the same.
The first to keep falsehood and lies
  far away from him, this,
    this I can ask for with no shame,
But to receive neither poverty nor riches? That I cannot claim.
  I went through that and I'm
Grateful you provided for each day,
  but I need a little more not to go astray.

It's not that I, like Midas, want my
  touch to turn to gold.
I know the problems greed and desire
  can cause among us people
    who tend to be quite bold.
But I still wonder if there can be more for me to hold.
  Like Tevye, I earnestly cry out
"Would it ruin some vast, eternal plan,
  if I had been born a wealthy man?"

I really just want more than nothing,
  to know my needs are met,
to know there's money for food, for fun,

      for books, for clothes, for rent.
        To not be in such debt.
But, perhaps that is the point. I'm not supposed to fret.
      You know that times have changed,
And that I need more to not be misled,
      than just some daily bread.

CHRISTINA VAN STARKENBURG

THE RIVER OF LIFE

All streams flow into the sea, yet the sea is never full. To the place the streams come from, there they return again.
Ecclesiastes 1:7

All streams flow into the sea.
Yet, the sea is never full.
The water simply joins the sky,
And travels to and fro.

We are like these little drops,
Falling from the sky.
Each time they splatter down anew.
No memory of their previous try.

Though we humans come and go,
Our Lord is a constant source.
He remembers each path we bore
As we trickled through the turf.

And so, it is good to trust in him
Who knows the past and every bend
Of the rivers we live in.
They all open before him in the end.

A LOVE POEM

Like an apple tree among the trees of the forest is my beloved among the young men.
Song of Songs 2:3

In the garden, I hunger to be found
By the one whose lush kisses warm my lips.
The scent of him always leaves me spellbound
When his tender arms wrap around my hips.
Through the night I miss his comforting touch,
Word of love filling my heart to the brim.
Alone and cold, I know I won't sleep much,
Instead, I rise and go to look for him.
Like an apple tree hiding in the pines,
He is concealed by all the young men.
But he enjoys plucking grapes from their vines,
So, I run through the streets to the garden.
There we embrace surrounded by flowers,
Our kisses become sensuous showers.

Part Four:
Major Prophets

DIRECTIONALLY CHALLENGED

The people walking in darkness have seen a great light; on those living in the land of deep darkness a light has dawned.
Isaiah 9:2

A voice calls out "Prepare the way!
Make straight the way for God!"

This voice, it echoes through the texts.
Isaiah, it points to you.

But, but we still stumble blindly.
Kicking pebbles with our feet.

We wave our hands in front of us,
And miss the signs we see.

Though we live in darkness,
A brand-new light has dawned.

The map towards our Saviour,
On Isaiah's lips was drawn.

Break the yoke that holds us,
Give us eyes to see.

Our Everlasting Father,
The promised Prince of Peace.

ON MY HEART

*"This is the covenant I will make with the house of Israel
after that time," declares the LORD.
"I will put my law in their minds
and write it on their hearts.
I will be their God,
and they will be my people.
No longer will they teach their neighbors,
or say to one another, 'Know the LORD,'
because they will all know me,
from the least of them to the greatest,"
declares the Lord.
Jeremiah 31:33-34*

        Our Father who art in heaven,
            We come to Thee today
        To step into the covenant
            You promised you would make.

        Place your law inside our minds,
            Burn it on our hearts.
        Let us know you personally,
            Have your Spirit leave a mark.

Coral on the Stone: A Lament

I called on your name, LORD, from the depths of the pit.
You heard my plea: "Do not close your ears to my cry for relief."

You came near when I called you, and you said, "Do not fear."
Lamentations 3:55-57

O God,

Do you look around and see?
   See the way it hurts?
Or is this my punishment from you,
   For my role in the curse?
Those I trusted with my life
   Are no where to be found.
Sailing off to some forsaken spot
   Leaving me here, alone, to drown.
It breaks, my soul, inside my heart.
   I feel so alone.
Without your touch upon my life
   I'm shattered like coral on the stone.

Yet even here, I think of you.
   I reel you in my mind.
Your great love washes over me,
   Your compassion floods my soul.
Like the tide covering green anemones again,
   Your faithfulness sustains.

It is good to wait. Patiently.
   For the salvation of my God.
It is good to hope in you,
   The Lord who can fix the shattered bone.

For Your Holy Name

"I had concern for my holy name, which the house of Israel profaned among the nations where they had gone."
Ezekiel 36:21

We trek through the mud when we carry your name
Careless as splatters mar and defame
People see us and think of you with a laugh
"Surely their god is worthless if he'd allow that."

Enough is enough. You will set everything right
The people on earth will see you in a new light.
No longer will we be scattered miles from home
You'll bring us back, burning everything but love for you alone.

Your name is holy. It should be treated as such.
We should wrap it in cloth to protect it from the muck.
Our actions should show we honour your name.
You can do it alone, but we should do the same.

FAITHFUL AND TRUE

Now when Daniel learned that the decree had been published, he home to his upstairs room where the windows opened toward Jerusalem. Three times a day he got down on his knees and prayed, giving thanks to his God, just as he had done before.
Daniel 6:10

The wicked plots of wicked men
Found no fault to expose in him
They gathered in hushed confab
Conjuring up a vicious plan
No man could pray to any being
Except their earthly mortal king

Daniel knew that what you said
Was more important than the rules of men
He knew—he heard—his king's decree
But your word was more important eternally

He bowed his head,
And bent his knee,
He turned towards you faithfully.

The lions' den
Loomed ahead.
Dark and bleak.
It was loud.
And it did reek.
But Daniel, he was not afraid

He trusted you, as he had always.
Though his body might be spent
Obedience was more important.

Daniel spent a silent night
Resting on a lion's might
The cats once fierce
For him just purred.

In the morning, he rose as a sign
You were power
You were kind
You intervened
Changed a king's mind.

Let my life be like Daniel's
Free from the reproach of men
Let there be no ghosts to find
No way to gain the upper hand

If they chose to target me through you
Help me to stay faithful and true
Fight your battle with my foes
So others may see the God that I chose.

Part Five:
The Book of the Twelve

Covenantal Rain

For I desire mercy, not sacrifice, and acknowledgment of God rather than burnt offerings.
Hosea 6:6

A covenant was made
When the world began
But, like a faithless bride
We wander when we can

Just like Adam, we always break
The covenant you long to remake
You desperately want us back
You love us deeply
With all that you have
But we choose to turn away
Because we think it's more fun to stray

More fun, until the good times end
And your judgements reign like the sun
But not yet, not today, not right at this hour
You wait, you watch, you warn
Reminding us of your mercy

Mercy, is what your heart craves
If we would acknowledge you
With our words and our ways
Then, once again, your love will rain.

Rend Your Heart

Rend your heart and not your garments. Return to the LORD your God, for he is gracious and compassionate, slow to anger and abounding in love, and he relents from sending calamity.
Joel 2:13

Rend your heart.

Not your garments.
Outward signs fall short.
Too easily faked.
For fame, for glory.
Lip service.
Not a sign of inner turmoil.

Rend your heart.

Take a knife
Cut away all that cuts asunder
Weep. Fast. Mourn.
Return.
Turn to the Lord your God.

Rend your heart.

All you people.
Young and old.
Women and men.
Church leaders, simple congregants.

Rend your heart.
Not your garments.
And He will be gracious
Welcome you once again.

JUST ASH

Seek good, not evil, that you may live. Then the LORD God Almighty will be with you, just as you say he is. Hate evil, love good; maintain justice in the courts. Perhaps the LORD God Almighty will have mercy on the remnant of Joseph.
Amos 5:14-15

With tinder tongues we burn to ash
The poor we cheat in courts of law
We kindle myths for gifts of cash
Blow air on flames with fibbing maws
We say "Of course it's what we saw
Why would we lie about it all?"
Falsehoods we will never withdraw
But, God is named God Who Rules Over All

He speaks to us with words that splash
Wet wisdom on our lying jaw
Douses greed in a painful flash
Our distortions we must withdraw
Rekindle justice with the law
Protect the poor who need not fall
God wants our frozen hearts to thaw
For God is the God Who Rules Over All

The Bystander Effect

On the day you stood aloof while strangers carried off his wealth and foreigners entered his gates and cast lots for Jerusalem, you were like one of them.
Obadiah 1:11

Oh Lord,

When we watch and wait and listen
Think someone else will call
Or worse, join in the jeering
You are wholly appalled.

To rejoice in their misfortune
Standing aside while they are harmed
This is not how you made us
But it is how we've become

Let us beg them for forgiveness
Let us bow our heads to you
And stand beside them;
they're our brethren
Help us defend them like you do.

LOVE OUR WAYWARD FEET

But Jonah ran away from the LORD *and headed for Tarshish. He went down to Joppa, where he found a ship bound for that port. After paying the fare, he went aboard and sailed for Tarshish to flee from the* LORD.
Jonah 1:3

Dear Lord

Through fierce storms
And waters deep
You watch every pattering
Of our wayward feet.

Your gift of love
You long to share
With neighbours, strangers
Everywhere.

Yet we, like Jonah,
Long to keep
This sacred treasure
As our own treat.

Dear Father up above
Flood us with your unfailing love.
Let us spread it far and near
So all will know they're welcome here.

MICAH 6:8

He has shown all you people what is good.
And what does the LORD require of you?
To act justly and to love mercy
and to walk humbly with your God.
Micah 6:8

Act Justly

Help us feed the poor
Sit with the sick and dying
Have integrity
Find justice for the abused
Defend the innocent ones

Love Mercy

Help us act with love
Be kind to those around us
Listen when they speak
Forgive those who have hurt us
Do a chore our loved ones hate

Walk Humbly with Your God

When we kneel 'fore you
Help us admit we need you
Every single day
Help us open up your word
Teach us once again to pray

JUDGEMENT/COMFORT

The Lord is slow to anger but great in power;
the Lord will not leave the guilty unpunished.
His way is in the whirlwind and the storm,
and clouds; are the dust of his feet.
Nahum 1:3[2]

There's no hope
No longer will I say
He brings comfort
I know
He only serves judgement
And
They cry out in vain
It's not true that
He cares
The Lord is against them
Don't try to convince me that
He'll relent

Now read it from the bottom up

---

[2] While I have this marked out as the theme verse, which usually means it's one of the verses that inspired the poem. That's not actually the case. I don't know if any of you have read all of Nahum, but it's right up there beside Obadiah as a depressing read.

However, as I was trying to figure out what to say, I learned that Nahum means comforter. And that inspired me to try to write a poem that says two very different messages depending on how you read it. So, please read this poem from top to bottom and then from the bottom to the top.

He'll relent
Don't try to convince me that
The Lord is against them
He cares
It's not true that
They cry out in vain
And
He only serves judgement
I know
He brings comfort
No longer will I say
There's no hope

Carrier Pigeon Prayers

I will stand at my watch and station myself on the ramparts; I will look to see what he will say to me, and what answer I am to give to this complaint.
Habakkuk 2:1

With broken words on pigeon wings
I mail my message to you.
As I watch it fly away
I hope my prayer's aim is true.
Now with nothing else to do,
At least, with nothing else I know,
I stand here on top of my roof
Ready, alert, and waiting
Looking for a response from you.
How long must this vigil last?
When will your word break through?
I grow weary, tired, and faint.
But still, I watch for you.
For days on end, I stand on guard
Until I spy your bird in flight.
My tired soul is filled with joy
When beside me it alights.
With faltering fingers, I undo
The clasp that binds the message to its feet
Unwinding the scroll, I brace my heart
And this is what I read:
"Revelation awaits on appointed time.
Though it lingers, wait for it.
It will come, and not delay."

CHILD'S PLAY

Then I will purify the lips of the peoples,
that all of them may call on the name of the LORD
and serve him shoulder to shoulder.
Zephaniah 3:9

Just watch the children
    as they try to make a blanket fort
Together, they push and pull the furniture
    to where it suits their needs
Then, each one grabs a blanket
    (sometimes two or three)
They discuss, and plan, and ponder
    where the blankets might work best
Carefully they try it out.
    Sometimes with failure, sometimes with success.
But when those blankets fall again,
    the kids bounce back with ease
Once more they try to figure out
    how to make them suit their needs
We should try to emulate
    their happy disposition
When we serve with each other
    whatever God has made our mission.

CHRISTINA VAN STARKENBURG

PALACE OF MUCK

Then the word of the LORD *came through the prophet Haggai:
"Is it a time for you yourselves to be living in your paneled
houses, while this house remains a ruin?"*
Haggai 1:3-4

Give careful thought to all your ways.
Don't expect too much.
If in a palace is where you dwell.
But you only give God a bit of muck.

Give careful thought to all your ways
If a blessing is what you desire.
Give God the best in all you can,
Show him your love is a bright fire.

LEAD-COVERED BASKET

Then the angel who was speaking to me came forward and said to me, "Look up and see what is appearing."

I asked, "What is it?"

He replied, "It is a basket." And he added, "This is the iniquity of the people throughout the land."

Then the cover of lead was raised, and there in the basket sat a woman!
Zechariah 5:5-7

God, our Father, maker of all the earth
You have lived each day
Your memory encompasses all time
Dementia and amnesia hold no sway

You will bring justice to those who oppress,
Evil won't survive
Stuffed into a basket covered with lead
It will await its prophesized demise

The wounded won't stay lying on the floor
They will be restored
The aged, with their chosen canes, will dance
With children in the streets to your hymn's chord

Nothing is every forgotten by you
You notice all things
Every memory stays fresh like it's new

Christina Van Starkenburg

Honor and glory to the king of kings

How Have I Loved You?[3]

"I have loved you," says the LORD.

"But you ask, 'How have you loved us?'"
Malachi 1:2a

How have I loved you? Let me count the ways.
Before time began, I gave you my name.
When you fell short, I cleansed all of your shame.
I promise to love you all of your days.
When you threw broken offerings in the flame,
I stepped in, sheltered you, and took the blame.
I love you freely. I give all I own.
My earth is a garden. Its food sustains.
I love you deeply. Canals in your bone
Carry my love to your heart through your veins.
I love you purely. My blood, this has shown.
My broken body, shattered all of your chains.
How have I loved you? Let me count the ways.
I'll show you new gifts, for all of your days.

---

[3] For those of you who are curious, this poem was also inspired by Elizabeth Barret Browning's sonnet "How Do I Love Thee?"

About the Author

Christina Van Starkenburg lives on the Canadian West Coast with her husband, two sons, daughter, and cat.

If you loved this collection of poetry, be sure to leave a star rating on Amazon, and sign up for her newsletter at www.christinavanstarkenburg.com so you can receive a new poem in your inbox every week.

Also, feel free to leave her a message on Instagram @christinavanstarkenburg or Facebook @christinavanstarkenburg.

Manufactured by Amazon.ca
Bolton, ON